It's A Money thing!

A GIRL'S GUIDE TO MANAGING MONEY

BY THE WOMEN'S FOUNDATION OF CALIFORNIA

ILLUSTRATED BY SUSAN ESTELLE KWAS

chronicle books · san francisco

I don't remember anyone teaching me about money as a young girl. In fact, I think conversations around money were limited to admonitions about spending wisely, saving coupons, and the virtues of thriftiness. It wasn't until I was 34, suddenly single, and the mother of three, that I learned how important it was to be knowledgeable about money matters—how to earn, spend, save, and invest money so that it worked for me. Today, I not only successfully manage my own money, but I provide guidance to others about how to manage their earnings and investments.

There are two things I know for sure about being financially savvy. First, knowledge is power. The more you know about how money works, the better you'll be at actually making money work for you. Second, it's never too early to start learning about how to manage money. In fact, the more you know now, the more fiscally healthy you'll be in the future.

That's where *It's a Money Thing!* comes in. This book was designed for you by women who know what it means to be empowered by money smarts. Each chapter was thoughtfully crafted with tips, tools, and fun activities to guide you through thinking about the role money plays in your life. With this resource in hand you are on the road to discovering how to make smart choices about money— knowledge that will serve you in every aspect of your life. Good luck on your journey!

—Kathleen Brown

Former treasurer of the State of California

Current head of the Public Sector and Infrastructure Group, Western Region, Goldman Sachs

CONTENTS

CHapter 1

You're at a party, wearing something fabulous made in Japan. Nibbling something yummy—raspberry cupcakes, perhaps?—you chance a smile or two at the cute stranger in the corner. Just as you're thinking of walking over in your fabulous new sandals, your best friend breezes by for a chat. After a bit of small talk, she casually asks if you've been watching the stock market lately. You almost choke mid-cupcake. The *what*? On and on she goes about the Dow this, the S&P that—when did your girl turn into Maria Bartiromo? (Not sure who she is? Look her up!)

OK, so maybe your friends are more likely to talk about iPods than iBonds, but it could happen. And yes, there are far better reasons to be money smart than intelligent party conversation. The fact is, we are all part of a global market place, buying, selling, and trading products that come from as far away as you can imagine—hello, fabulous sandals!—and as close as the bakery on the corner. Understanding the ebbs and flows of commerce just makes good sense.

That's where *It's a Money Thing!* comes in. This book offers a chance for you to think about your role in the global market-place, to imagine and play, so that when the good life comes knocking, you'll be ready to open the door wide.

A few things to keep in mind as you read this book:

· You know how your grandparents wax nostalgic about penny candy and movies that cost a quarter? Clearly things change over time. While we've done our very best to make the information in this book as up-to-date as possible, keep in mind that the salaries, costs, and other such things are averages, and can fluctuate from year to year. By giving you these numbers we're painting a general picture of the world we live in so that you can begin to think about your place in it.

· The examples in this book are just that: examples. They're meant to show how the choices you make now can affect your financial future. We can't promise that if you follow our advice step by step you'll get the exact same results, but we are offering essential guidelines you need to be smart about your money. There is so much more to know about money than we can offer in the scope of this book, so please check the resources in the back for more information.

· There are few things people get more emotional about than money. That's why at the end of every chapter we've offered a chance for you to write down your thoughts about what you just learned. Don't feel confined by those few pages. Use them as a starting point, grab your own journal, and write on!

your favorite

SHOP

jouRNal

How do you participate in the global market every day?

Let's start right where you are. Use the following journal pages to keep track of everything you buy this week and how much it cost, and then read the label to find out where it came from.

	I BOUGHT	IT COST	IT CAME FROM
MONDAY			
TUESDAY			
WEDNESDAY			
THURSDAY			
FRIDAY			
SATURDAY			
SUNDAY			

As you gather the info for this chart, choose an accounting style that works best for you:

- Carry this book with you and record your information right away.
- Keep a slip of paper in your wallet to jot down the facts each time you buy something.
- Hold on to your receipts and record the facts at the end of each day.
- Keep track of your purchases in a spreadsheet program like Excel.

	I BOUGHT	IT COST	IT CAME FROM
MONDAY			
TUESDAY			
WEDNESDAY			
THURSDAY			
FRIDAY			
SATURDAY			
SUNDAY			

journal

Now get out your
calculator and add it up!

How many different places did the products you purchased come from?

How much money did you spend this week?

Is there anything that surprised you about your spending habits?

Is there anything you would like to change about your spending habits?

chapter 2

One of the easiest ways to become part of the global financial market (aside from shopping) is to start a business of your own. Think you're too young? You probably already have the creativity and smarts to be an **entrepreneur**. Check out these girls who went into business for themselves when they were about your age:

Shantol Henry: 16, from Queens, New York. When the snack shop at her school was shut down, Shantol founded The Candy Confection, a company based in her school that creates, packages, and sells candy, and also mentors other students to learn about running their own businesses.

Weina Scott: 17, from North Miami Beach, Florida. Weina used her passion for computers to create Switchpod.com, which provides users with space to upload audio and video programs as podcasts.

Annie Torres: 18, from Redwood City, California. Annie founded Annie's Vals, a business that teaches girls the special waltz that is a key part of the *quinceañera* celebration.

How did they do it? Let's take a look at this story of a young girl with a dog and a dream.

Once upon a time, Maria—a rather independent sort—was tired of always asking her parents for money. She picked up a little cash here and there doing odd jobs, but she was over mowing lawns and changing diapers. Besides, she wanted something more steady, and as a 14-year-old, she was having a hard time getting a job at the businesses in her neighborhood. So she decided to start a business of her own.

Brainstorming

Maria had no idea what kind of business she wanted to start, but she made a list of the things that interested her:

Softball

Ballet

Baking

Swimming

Taking care of Mr. Pockets

Helping my friends with homework

Watching TV

Shopping

Reading to Mrs. Nelson

She took a look at the list and tried to imagine how she might turn each item into a business:

Softball:
I could work with a Little League team. (But would I have to volunteer? And what will I do when the season is over?)

Ballet: ?

Baking:
I do like experimenting in the kitchen. (But I want to be outside!)

Swimming: ?

Taking care of Mr. Pockets:
Maybe dog walking?

Helping my friends with homework:
I could start a tutoring service . . .

Watching TV: ?

Shopping: ?

Reading to Mrs. Nelson:
Would people pay me to read to them?

Brainstorming like this helped her eliminate a few things immediately:

~~Softball:~~
~~I could work with a Little League team. (But would I have to volunteer? And what will I do when the season is over?)~~

~~Ballet: ?~~

~~Baking:~~
~~I do like experimenting in the kitchen. (But I want to be outside!)~~

~~Swimming~~ ?

Taking care of Mr. Pockets:
  Maybe dog walking?

Helping my friends
with homework:
  I could start a tutoring service . . .

~~Watching TV~~ ?

~~Shopping~~ ?

~~Reading to Mrs. Nelson~~:
  ~~Would people pay
  me to read to them~~?

When Maria looked at her list again, she realized that as much as she liked helping her friends, the thought of how many students she'd have to tutor to really make money didn't appeal to her. But the idea of a dog-walking service seemed just right.

YOUR TURN

Ready to make a list like Maria's? In the space below write down ten things that interest you. Anything goes in this first pass.

1.

2.

3.

4.

5.

6.

7.

8.

9.

10.

Now take a look at your list again. Is there anything you can eliminate?

You've Got Skills

Maria was a natural with dogs. Mr. Pockets had been with her since he was a puppy, and she was the one who taught him how to sit, stay, and fetch. (Her brother liked to take credit for teaching him to play dead.) Plus, she was naturally athletic and felt she could easily manage a pack of pups and chase after any who strayed. But was there a need for a dog walker in her neighborhood?

YOUR TURN

As you narrow your list, think about the skills you already have that might help your business. Are you a math ace? Artistic? Good with people? Are there skills you need to learn? (How to keep your cheesecakes from cracking, for example.) If so, will you take classes? Find a mentor? (Give up cheesecakes and make brownies instead?)

Market Research

There were a lot of dogs in Maria's neighborhood, so it stood to reason that there was a need for a dog walker. Plus, there were a lot of elderly dog owners who might appreciate the extra help.

To test her hunch, Maria had a chat with Mr. Jones, an 80-year-old man who lived three doors down. Mr. Jones liked the idea of having Maria walk his dog, Chester, and told her about several other elderly people in the neigh-borhood who'd pay for a dog-walking service. He also knew of several people who worked during the day and would like to have their dogs walked in the afternoon. Maria knocked on a few more doors and found that people were desperate for a dog walker and were more than willing to pay for the service. And with that, Maria finished her first round of **market research**. There would certainly be more to come.

> **MARKET RESEARCH:**
> *research that determines whether there's a need (or market) for a particular service, and what the competition, if any, might be*

YOUR TURN

How's your list of business ideas looking? Have you narrowed it down to one or two possibilities? What kind of research can you do to find out if there's a need for your business?

The Name Game

Now that Maria knew her business would be a hit, she had to figure out what to call it. Here's what she came up with:

Maria's Mutts
(Hmm…Sounds like I'm selling unwanted pups…)

Doggone Walking Service
(Eh.)

Bowwow Buddies
(Possibilities…)

The Woof-Woof Walker
(Maybe just a little too cute…)

With the help of her friends, her family, and her own instincts, Maria decided to go with Bowwow Buddies.

YOUR TURN

What would you like to name your business? Make a list of possibilities, then pick a name you feel great about and test it out on your family and friends.

1.

2.

3.

4.

Mission: Possible

Maria knew that the clearer she was about the purpose of her company, the easier it would be for her to keep her focus and to explain to other people what she is all about. Here's the **mission statement** she came up with:

> **MISSION STATEMENT:**
> *a written description of a company that clearly outlines its purpose and sometimes its goals*

Bowwow Buddies will provide a dog-walking service to people in the community who are not able to walk their own dogs. The company will help the dogs by providing daily exercise and it will help the owners by alleviating concerns about their beloved pets.

YOUR TURN

Take a stab at writing a mission statement for your business. What will your business do? How will it benefit customers?

My Mission Statement:

18

Getting Goal-Oriented

Now that Maria had a clear mission statement, she was ready to outline some goals for her business. Some of her goals were more immediate. Others were more long-term:

1. Provide a daily dog-walking service to the local community.

2. Provide this service to the elderly in the community who are not physically able to walk their dogs and to working people who aren't home in the afternoons.

3. Within three months of starting the service, I will provide daily walks for six dogs. I will walk three dogs per hour.

YOUR TURN

Write down what you will do, who your customers will be, and what you want your business to be providing three months from now.

Goals for My Business:

1.

2.

3.

4.

Create a Marketing and Sales Plan

Just about everything was in place for Maria's business to be a success: There was a need for her business, it combined her interests and skills, and she had a clear mission and goals. And of course, there was the catchy name. It was time to get the word out about Bowwow Buddies, so she developed a marketing and sales plan:

1. *Ask around and find potential customers in the neighborhood.*

2. *Design and photocopy flyers to advertise Bowwow Buddies.*

3. *Distribute flyers to neighbors' houses, the local senior center, train station, and local grocery stores.*

4. *After working with my first client, ask for a letter of recommendation. Then redesign the flyers to include the positive quotes from the letter.*

5. *Ask for letters from every satisfied customer, to add testimonial quotes to my flyers.*

YOUR TURN

What steps can you take to advertise your business to the right audience? Write them down here.

My Marketing and Sales Plan:

1.

2.

3.

4.

5.

Identify the
Resources You'll Need

What materials did Maria need to make Bowwow Buddies a success? She made yet another list:

1. *This is a one-person operation, unless I expand later, so I don't need any staff right now.*

2. *Two leashes with collar. Each owner will probably have a leash, but I should have extras, just in case an owner can't find one.*

3. *Dog biscuits—one box a week.*

4. *Pooper-scooper bags.*

YOUR TURN

What human resources and materials will you need for your business? Make a list:

1.

2.

3.

4.

5.

It Takes Money to Make Money

As she was compiling all of her notes and imagining what it would be like when the cash started rolling in, it occurred to Maria that starting a business takes money. She was going to have to buy those leashes and pooper-scooper bags somehow. So she flipped a page in her notebook and wrote out another list:

Bowwow Buddies Budget
(Expenses for Maximum Six Dogs)

INITIAL START-UP COSTS

Leashes:	$20
Flyers:	$10
Total start-up expense:	**$30**

WEEKLY EXPENSES

Dog biscuits:	$5/week
Pooper-scooper bags:	$3/week
Total weekly expense:	**$8/week**

WEEKLY INCOME (MAXIMUM 6 DOGS PER WEEK)

$10 per 6 dogs per week	$60
Minus weekly expenses	$8
Total weekly income (profit)	$52

After earning back start-up costs, Maria figured that Bowwow Buddies would make $52 a week in profits—that's about $2,700 a year!

Now follow Maria's lead and make a budget for your business:

NAME OF BUSINESS ....

Start-Up Expenses

ITEM	AMOUNT
	$
	$
TOTAL START-UP EXPENSE	$

Weekly Expenses

ITEM	AMOUNT
	$
	$
	$
TOTAL WEEKLY EXPENSE	$
WEEKLY INCOME	$
MINUS WEEKLY EXPENSES	$
TOTAL WEEKLY INCOME (PROFIT)	$

After your expenses are paid, are you making a profit that satisfies you? If not, you can figure out how to cut down on your expenses and/or charge more for your product.

Create a Launch Calendar

Ever organized, Maria put her book of lists away, grabbed a wall calendar, and planned out each step of her business plan.

JUNE week 1	*Make flyers and business cards* *Go shopping for dog biscuits and pooper-scooper bags*
JUNE week 2	*Knock on doors to sign up customers and post flyers around the neighborhood*
JUNE week 3	*Make a list of customers, the names of their dogs, and the dates and times of their appointments.* *Start walking those dogs! (If I can sign up some customers.)*
JUNE week 4	*Ask new customers for letters of recommendation. Create and post new flyers with endorsements from happy customers.* *Go shopping for more supplies, if necessary*

YOUR TURN

Find a wall or pocket calendar (or draw your own) and imagine the things you'll need to do to start up and run your business.

Dear Diary

Maria's business was really taking off! She decided to keep a diary of her progress and all of the things she did along the way:

Saturday, March 6

Distributed 30 flyers at the Senior Citizens' Center and with Mrs. Gibb, the director. She said she'd make an announcement about Bowwow Buddies at all the senior group meetings. Went home and wrote her a thank-you note.

The notebook that once held all of her lists now became a place for her to keep track of all the business conversations she had about Bowwow Buddies, what she learned, and what was decided. She recorded her conversation with Mrs. Gibb there, for example. Here she had a record of all the contacts she'd made, including their telephone numbers and e-mail addresses. She also had a history of her business that she could look back at when she wanted to recall why she decided to do one thing and not another. This was now her marketing log.

In another notebook, Maria kept track of her finances. She tallied her spending and the money her customers paid her. Remembering that her parents were always pulling out shoeboxes of receipts come tax time, she also kept all of her receipts.

Every week, Maria reviewed her business diary, her marketing notebook, and her financial notebook.

YOUR TURN

Maria liked keeping many notebooks and lists, but you can keep all of this information in one diary, if you'd like. Or you can keep separate notebooks just like Ms. M.

Evaluation

After three months, Bowwow Buddies seemed to be successful, but Maria wanted to check in to be sure. She asked herself these questions:

1. Am I fulfilling my mission statement?
2. Am I meeting my goals?
3. How much money is my company making?
4. What obstacles have I faced?
5. If I were to start my business over, what would I do differently?

As she answered these questions, Maria discovered she could improve on a few things.

For instance, when she first started out, she didn't even think about how the weather might affect her business. People really wanted someone to walk their dog when the weather was rotten, but on all of the gorgeous, sunny days they had that spring, most dog owners saw walking their dogs as a way to get out and enjoy the weather. While Maria wasn't thrilled about being out in the rain with six dogs, she knew her business would be better when the weather was bad. She needed to factor a certain number of sunny days into her budget. On those days she wasn't likely to make any money.

Even with the weather concerns, Maria's evaluation told her that her business was successful. With all of her planning, how could she fail? She decided to celebrate by buying a CD by her favorite band.

The End.

Now let's suppose you start a business and it's successful like Maria's. What will you do with the money you earn? The next few chapters will give you some ideas.

jOurNal

Successful businesses come in all shapes and sizes. Some stay very small and local, while others expand to become national or international corporations. What would you prefer for your business? Why?

Chapter 3

Now assuming the business you start doesn't make you a multi-millionaire (and even if it does), we need to take a moment here to talk about staying in school. You've heard it before, and you know it's true: education equals money. Of course, there are some jobs where experience is more important than the number of years you spent in school, but generally speaking, the more advanced your degree, the greater your earning potential, and the better prepared you are to take a swing at life's curveballs. Besides, there are few things more powerful than an educated woman.

Here's how your years in school can translate into dollars and cents:

LEVEL OF EDUCATION	AVERAGE EARNINGS*
Less than 9th grade	$17,422
Not a high school graduate	$20,321
High school graduate	$26,505
Associate degree	$35,009
Bachelor's degree	$43,143
Master's degree	$52,390
Doctorate	$70,853
Professional degree	$82,473

*DATA FROM U.S. CENSUS BUREAU. EDUCATIONAL ATTAINMENT—PEOPLE 25 YEARS OLD AND OVER BY TOTAL MONEY EARNINGS IN 2005; CURRENT POPULATION SURVEY, AUGUST 2006

"**Women comprise 56% of Americans over 18 who live in poverty. Yet, women's earnings and income increase dramatically when they have college degrees.**"

—CAROL HOLLENSHEAD,
DIRECTOR OF THE CENTER FOR THE EDUCATION OF WOMEN, UNIVERSITY OF MICHIGAN

Of course, some professions require a little more training than others. For example:

POSITION	EDUCATION*
ACCOUNTANT	Bachelor's degree with an emphasis on accounting and finance
ADVERTISING SALESPERSON	Bachelor's degree
ARCHITECT	Bachelor's of architecture, or a Master's of architecture and a license to practice
CHILD-CARE WORKER	Varies by state. Minimum requirement: high school diploma
COMPUTER PROGRAMMER	Bachelor's degree in computer science or information systems
CUSTOMER-SERVICE REP	High school diploma
DOCTOR (GENERAL PRACTICE)	Bachelor's in pre-med, plus doctorate of medicine and a three- to eight-year internship or residency
ELECTRICIAN	High school diploma or GED and apprenticeship

POSITION	EDUCATION*
ELEMENTARY SCHOOL TEACHER	Bachelor's degree in education and license to teach
GRAPHIC DESIGNER	Bachelor's degree in fine arts and graphic design
HAIRDRESSER	High school or GED and graduation from a licensed cosmetology school and a state license to practice
LAWYER	Graduate degree from an accredited law school and pass the state bar examination
LIBRARIAN	Master's degree in library science
RECEPTIONIST	High school diploma or GED
RETAIL SALESPERSON	No formal degree, some training required
SOCIAL WORKER	Bachelor's degree in social work
VETERINARIAN	Doctorate in veterinary science and a license to practice

*DATA FROM U.S. CENSUS BUREAU, EDUCATIONAL ATTAINMENT—PEOPLE 25 YEARS OLD AND OVER BY TOTAL MONEY EARNINGS IN 2005, CURRENT POPULATION SURVEY, AUGUST 2006

And how much money can that training translate into?

OCCUPATION	AVERAGE SALARY*
Accountant	$56,389
Advertising salesperson	$48,173
Architect	$70,506
Child-care worker	$20,267
Computer programmer	$74,142
Customer-service rep	$31,563
Doctor (general practice)	$139,091
Electrician	$47,349
Elementary school teacher	$53,081
Graphic designer	$44,706
Hairdresser	$19,919
Receptionist	$24,214
Lawyer	$121,309
Librarian	$58,753
Retail salesperson	$20,682
Social worker	$43,900
Veterinarian	$82,364

*DATA FROM THE CALIFORNIA OCCUPATIONAL EMPLOYMENT AND STATISTICS SURVEY 2006

Pretty interesting, isn't it? Not that your career choice should be all about your bank account. People are generally happiest when they make a career out of something they love (see Chapter 7). And even if following your dreams doesn't make you a millionaire, It's a Money Thing! will show you how to turn even modest earnings into the life you deserve.

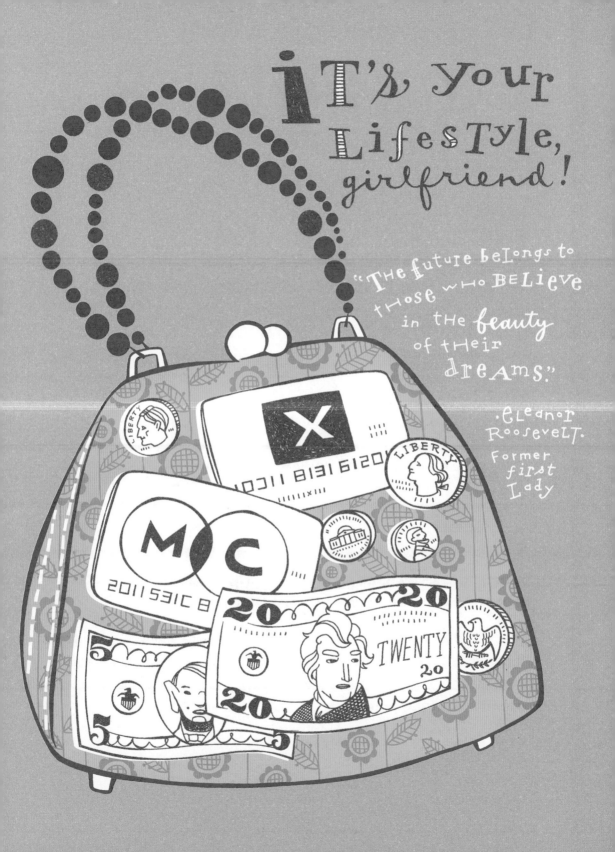

iT's your LifesTyle, girlfriend!

"The future beLongs to those who BeLieve in the *beauty* of their *dreams*."

·eLeanor RooseveLT. Former *first* Lady

L et's imagine you've studied hard, you're out of school, and you've just landed the job of your dreams. Your new annual salary is $28,000. Let's assume there are 26 pay periods in a year (one every other week). That means you should be getting about $1,077 a paycheck, right? Well, here's your first one:

DREAM JOB, INC.
9 CLOUD LANE
SILVER LINING, USA 54321

1234567

DATE *Today*

PAY TO THE
ORDER OF: *You*

$518.38

THIS AMOUNT:
five hundred eighteen and ³⁸/₁₀₀ dollars

Your Boss

CITYBANKS
RICHLAND, USA

AUTHORIZED SIGNATURE

WHOA! WHAT HAPPENED TO ALL YOUR MONEY? DON'T PANIC. HERE'S WHAT'S GOING ON:

That $28,000 you were promised when you were hired is your **gross income**. But thanks to Uncle Sam and other organizations that require a little bit of money from everyone, the money that actually goes into your pocket—your **take-home pay**—is a lot less than $28K.

FIT: Federal Income Tax

Remember how upset the colonists were way back when, when a tax was placed on their tea? Taxes are here to stay, no matter how much you'd like to protest by chucking things into large bodies of water. (You wouldn't want to do that anyway—bad for the environment.)

Income tax is money the United States government automatically takes from everyone's paycheck to pay for military expenses, elected officials' salaries, welfare programs, medical research, food inspectors, and national parks, among other things. Of all the money that is deducted from your gross income, the largest amount is eaten up by taxes, but the amount varies depending on how much money you make. If you earn $24,600 or under per year, 15% of your income is deducted for taxes. If you earn between $24,600 and $60,000, 28% is deducted, and if you earn $60,000 or above, deductions are between 31 and 39.6%. If your salary is $28,000, your federal income tax for the whole year is $7,840.

Elected government officials make the final decisions
as to how income tax money is spent. Since they are
handling about one-third of your earnings, it's important
that you vote for people who you believe will make
good decisions spending it.

FICA: Federal Insurance Compensation Act

This is money invested by the government to pay for Social Security (your retirement income after age 65) and for Medicare, a health insurance program for retirees and disabled workers. Out of your total earnings, 6.2% (a maximum of $4,100) is used for Social Security, and 1.45% for Medicare. In our example, $1,736 will be deducted annually for Medicare, and $406 for Social Security.

SIT: State and Local Income Tax

Depending on where you live, your state and local government deducts between 0 and 9.3% of your income to pay for things such as schools, libraries, and public transportation. Let's just say you live in a state that deducts 7% income tax, and your local tax is 8%. This means you'll be paying $1,960 in state taxes and $2,244 in local.

UI: Unemployment Insurance

This 1.2% deduction is for money that is put aside for you to use if you're ever unemployed. It's a little bit to help you get by as you look for another job. Your annual deduction for unemployment insurance will be $336.

Health Insurance

One deduction we didn't mention in the take-home-pay example is health insurance. This is a program that covers a certain percentage of your medical expenses for a small cost. Until you're 21, you're probably covered on your parents' insurance plan, but after that, you're on your own. Most employers offer some insurance plan, and the amount they're willing to pay for your coverage (and the amount they require you to pay) varies from company to company. If your employer doesn't offer health insurance, you'll want to look into buying it for yourself. Even though you're young and healthy, it's good to be prepared for the unexpected.

If you add all of these deductions up, subtract them from $28,000 and divide that number by 26, you get $518.38. Mystery solved.

> *Keep in mind that we've mentioned the major deductions that everyone who earns a paycheck has to worry about. There are others that vary by state and by company. It can be a little scary to realize how much of your money is spent before you even see a dime. The key is to make the most of the money you do take home. That's where being money smart comes in.*

How far can you stretch your income? Let's take a look at the lifestyles of three very different young working women. First, the facts:

MISA works as an administrative assistant for a small software development company. Her salary is $24,000 a year. After taxes are taken out of her paycheck, she takes home about $1,600 a month. She sticks to a tight **budget** and saves around $5,100 per year.

JASMINE teaches fourth grade in a public school. She makes $37,000 a year. After taxes she takes home about $2,000 per month. At the end of the year, she has saved $4,800.

GABRIELLA is a lawyer who works for a mid-sized corporate law firm. She makes $66,000 a year. After taxes she takes home $3,850 per month. By the end of the year, she manages to save $300.

Do these numbers surprise you? How is it possible that Gabriella makes almost three times as much as Misa, yet Misa saves thousands of dollars more a year than Gabriella? The answer is that they have made different lifestyle choices.

Take a look at two big choices they each have made that affect their savings the most.

WHERE DO THEY CHOOSE TO LIVE?

MISA lives in a small apartment in a decent neighborhood where the rent is relatively inexpensive compared to other neighborhoods in the city. She has a roommate, and they split the $1,200 monthly rent.

JASMINE lives in a studio apartment in Misa's neighborhood. She lives alone and pays the entire rent, which comes to $900 a month.

GABRIELLA lives in a large apartment in an upscale neighborhood. She pays $2,000 a month in rent.

WHAT KIND OF TRANSPORTATION DO THEY CHOOSE?

MISA bought a used Toyota with cash. Even though she pays about $600 a year on repairs, she doesn't have any car payments.

JASMINE bought a new Jeep Wrangler and has car payments of about $350 a month.

GABRIELLA bought a Porsche and has payments of $900 a month.

Is the fact that Misa saves more than Gabriella starting to make sense? What if Gabriella made the same lifestyle choices as Misa? If Gabriella chose to have a roommate and to drive a used car, after a year she would save $22,500!

Keep in mind that in the examples above, only federal taxes were taken out of the women's paychecks. As you saw earlier in the chapter, in real life many more deductions are taken that vary from state to state, and company to company. Regardless of this, the saving principles are the same.

Enough about Misa, Gabriella, and Jasmine. Now let's talk about you.

Livin' the Good Life

When you're first living on your own, you'll probably start out by renting a place before you own. Ever thought of what kind of place you'd like to live in?

THINGS TO CONSIDER:

Are you a city girl?
Do you want to live in the suburbs?
Do you want roommates?
Would you rather live on your own?

SAVVY BUDGET GUIDELINE

Your monthly rent will be your biggest expense and should equal about 35 to 40% of your monthly income. Choose a job from the list in Chapter 2 that sounds interesting to you and let's figure out how much of your salary will go to your rent.

MY MONTHLY TAKE-HOME INCOME:

$

MONTHLY RENT EXPENSE GUIDELINE
(multiply monthly income by 0.35):

$

ACTUAL MONTHLY RENT OF MY APARTMENT:

$

Now that you've got a rough estimate of what you'll be able to afford, check this out:

SIZE	LOCATION	AVERAGE RENT
Studio	Manhattan, NY	$1,500
Studio	San Francisco, CA	$900
Studio	Other parts of the U.S.	$650
1 bedroom	Manhattan, NY	$2,400
1 bedroom	San Francisco, CA	$1,300
1 bedroom	Other parts of the U.S.	$950
2 bedroom	Manhattan, NY	$4,000
2 bedroom	San Francisco, CA	$2,200
2 bedroom	Other parts of the U.S.	$1,300

SOURCE: U.S. CENSUS BUREAU

 How does this information affect your thinking about where you'd like to live and the size of your apartment?

Other Housing Expenses

Living on your own, you'll also have your own phone, Internet access, and maybe a TV. You'll be paying for the energy it takes to keep your place lit up, heated, or air-conditioned. And depending on where you live, you might also have to pay for garbage pickup, and even water.

Sound overwhelming? There are definitely ways to cut down on expenses. For example, how would you feel about not having cable TV? If you have a cell phone, do you need a home phone too? Will you live in a part of the country where you can go without air conditioning?

Here are some averages for how much your other housing expenses will cost you each month:

GROCERIES **$200**	**HOME PHONE** **$40**	**CABLE** **$60**
UTILITIES (electricity, gas, and water) **$80**	**CELL PHONE** **$60**	

SOURCE: U.S. CENSUS BUREAU

Now that you've got an idea of where you'd like to live, and how much you'll probably pay for other household expenses, add it up:

TOTAL MONTHLY HOUSING EXPENSE	**$**

Hit the Road!

In a perfect world, cars would be cheap, fuel would be free, and no one would ever get parking tickets. In the real world, there are definitely ways to cut the costs of getting around town. The easiest way, of course, is to live close enough to work that you can walk or bike. (Good for the environment and your health!) But if you're like most people and work is a little farther than a mile or two, you'll probably either be taking public transit or driving.

First, let's tackle public transit. The cost for riding a city bus or train varies from place to place. For example:

CITY	
NEW YORK CITY	**$2.00** ($2.25 with transfer)
CHICAGO	**$2.00** $1.75 with transit card on buses
SAN FRANCISCO	**$1.50** (includes transfer)

SOURCES: U.S. MTA.INFO, YOURCTA.COM, SFMTA.COM

You've probably got your dream car all picked out, right? While you're thinking about leather seats and paint jobs, take a look at the list below. It'll give you a sense of how much different cars might cost you, assuming a down payment of between 10% and 30% of the retail price.

AVERAGE MONTHLY CAR PAYMENTS	
2007 VOLKSWAGEN JETTA	$358
2007 HONDA ACCORD COUPE	$374
2007 TOYOTA PRIUS	$448
2007 FORD EXPLORER	$510

SOURCE: JDPOWER.COM

In some cities, if you buy a transit card, monthly pass, or unlimited use pass, you can save some cash. For example, with a Chicago Card (a transit pass that deducts money from your credit or **debit card** every time you swipe it), a one-way ride on a Chicago bus or subway is $1.75. In San Francisco, a monthly pass will cost you $45, in New York City, $76. Plus, some employers will cover a certain percentage of your public transport costs. Definitely something to look into.

Now let's suppose you'd rather get behind the wheel than let someone else do the driving. If you're in the market for a new car, you'll probably need to take out a loan to pay for it. This just means that a bank—or some other lending institution—will agree to give you the money, but you'll have to repay it with **interest**. To decide whether you're a good candidate for a loan, banks will look at your credit history—to see how much **debt** you currently have, and to see whether you've been good about making your payments on time. One of the easiest ways for banks to tell if you have good credit history is to check out how responsible you are with your **credit card**. But if you're not careful, credit cards can be more dangerous than helpful.

What's with Credit Cards, Anyway?

Credit is a loan of money. Banks and other financial institutions issue credit cards so you can easily borrow money from them. Every time you swipe your card, you're promising to pay your credit card company back—with interest.

Credit card companies determine interest in terms of an **annual percentage rate (APR)**. Let's say you have a brand new, never-been-used-before credit card with an annual percentage rate of 20%. You decide you just cannot live without that $2,000 coat you saw in the window of your favorite shop, and you hand over your card. Thirty days later, you get a credit card bill that shows your $2,000 balance (the **principal**) and the minimum amount you have to pay. This amount is usually equal to a percentage of your balance, which varies, depending on the credit card company. Let's say your company requires that you pay a minimum of 3% of your balance each month. Doesn't sound like much, right? Here's the thing: Because your credit card's APR is 20%, your interest for that month is $33.33. That means when you get your bill, you'll owe $2,033 if you just decide to pay the minimum amount, here's where your money really goes:

PRINCIPAL: $2,000

MINIMUM PAYMENT REQUIRED: $60.00 (3% of $2,000)

INTEREST: $33.33 ((20% of $2,000) /12)

AMOUNT OF MINIMUM PAYMENT THAT GOES TOWARD PRINCIPAL: $26.67 ($60.00–$33.33)

REMAINING BALANCE: $1,973.33

So, even if you pay the minimum, less than half of it as actually going toward paying off your balance. And every month, your credit card company makes the same calculations until your debt is paid off. If you just pay the minimum on this balance, it will take you 15 years to pay for your coat, and in the end, you will have paid over $4,200.

If you must use credit cards, you're always better off paying more than the minimum balance, or paying off the balance in full before your bill even arrives. But the very best advice we can give is this: If you have to use a credit card to pay for something, chances are you really can't afford it, and credit card debt can be tough to get out of. So think hard before you charge.

Can I Get a Car Loan if I Don't Have a Credit Card?

Even though credit cards can be dangerous, if you use them wisely, they can help establish good credit. Good credit will help you get a car loan, or a loan for a house. Some landlords even require a credit check before they'll rent you an apartment. If you need a loan and you haven't established credit yet, you can ask a parent or someone who has good credit history to co-sign the loan for you.

As you know, there's more to having a car than just the payments on your loan. Check this out:

EXPENSE	AVG. MONTHLY COST
INSURANCE	$125
GAS	$100
REPAIRS (oil, maintenance)	$35

SOURCE: U.S. CENSUS BUREAU

Considering everything we've covered, what do you think your monthly transportation expenses might be? Use the space below to add it all up:

Monthly car payment	$
Monthly insurance payment	$
Monthly gas expense	$
Monthly public transportation expense	$
TOTAL MONTHLY TRANSPORTATION EXPENSE	$

Savvy Budget Guideline

Your monthly transportation expense should ideally be about 10% of your monthly income. Figure it out like this:

My monthly income (refer to Chapter 2)	$
Monthly transportation guideline (multiply monthly income by 0.10)	$
TOTAL MONTHLY TRANSPORTATION EXPENSE	$

Is your actual monthly transportation expense about the same as your monthly transportation expense guideline? If it's higher, you can consider choosing a lower-priced new car or finding a bargain on a used one. Or maybe that bike is looking better and better?

Bring on the fun

You've got your place, you've got your ride, now it's time to have a little fun. Using the chart you filled out in Chapter 1 and the list on the next page, think about how much money you might spend on all the things that make life more interesting.

SAVVY SAVings TiPs

INSTEAD OF . . .

Buying books and movies . . . check them out of the library for free.

Going out to a restaurant . . . throw a fabulous dinner party at your apartment and have all your friends bring their favorite dish.

Joining a gym . . . schedule weekly times with your girl-friends to jog or bike.

Buying gifts . . . make or bake presents for your friends and family.

Shopping at the mall . . . shop at second-hand stores or consignment shops.

SAVE

EXPENSE	COST
ONE MOVIE (not including snacks)	$11
ONE MUSEUM VISIT	$10
ONE RENTAL MOVIE	$5
ONE CD	$16
ONE DVD	$20
ONE LOCAL CONCERT	$25
ONE PAPERBACK BOOK	$16
ONE RESTAURANT MEAL	$20
MONTHLY GYM MEMBERSHIP	$50
ONE SPECIALTY COFFEE TO GO	$48 ($4 a pop, three times a week)
ONE SNACK TO GO	$36 ($3 a pop, three times a week)

SOURCE: U.S. CENSUS BUREAU

Now get out your calculator and add up what your total monthly entertainment expense will be.

Monthly activities (movies, concerts, gym, restaurants, travel)	$
Monthly fun purchases (CDs, DVDs, hobbies, gifts)	$
TOTAL MONTHLY ENTERTAINMENT EXPENSE	$

Looking
Good!

Can you live the good life without a fantastic wardrobe? Well, of course you can, but would it be as much fun?

Saving-savvy girls know how to hunt for bargains, pore though vintage racks, and look fantastic without spending a bundle. The average woman spends about $100 a month on clothes. How does your spending compare? What are you spending on makeup? Haircuts? Write the amount you think you might spend in the blanks below.

Monthly new clothes	$
Monthly new shoes	$
Accessories and jewelry	$
Dry-cleaning and laundry	$
Haircut	$
Makeup	$
TOTAL MONTHLY CLOTHING AND BEAUTY EXPENSE	$

Other Monthly Bills

You may have taken out a loan for college and are paying it off in monthly installments. And you may have a credit card bill to pay every month. Average monthly payments for these may be:

Student loan payment
$200

Credit card payment
$150

 Now get out your calculator and add up what your total other monthly bills will be.

Student loan payment	$
Credit card payment	$
TOTAL OTHER BILLS	$

Drumroll
Please...

You knew it was coming. It's time to look back at all of the figuring and calculating you've done so far and add it all up to determine your total monthly expenses:

MY LIFESTYLE CHOICES	ESTIMATED COSTS
My apartment (including utilities)	$
My transportation	$
My entertainment	$
My groceries and home supplies	$
My clothes and makeup	$
MY TOTAL MONTHLY EXPENSE	$

Congratulations! (Whew!)

"Financial security is the key to survival . . . confidence in what you do and who you are is the key to a successful life."
—NICKOLE COLLINS PIERRE, AGE 21

Save, Save, Save!

Until this point all we've talked about is spending and expenses, but we haven't mentioned the most important expense of all: You. If you save a little and invest each month, you'll find that your money goes further than you might have imagined. This is how you make your money stretch beyond just what you bring home at the end of each pay period.

As a rule of thumb, your savings should equal about 10% of your monthly take-home income. Let's figure out what that should be:

MY MONTHLY TAKE-HOME INCOME:
$

10% OF MY MONTHLY INCOME
(multiply income by 0.10):
$

Now let's see how much money you'll have left after your monthly expenses.

Before we talk about investing, let's see how much money you have to save:				
YOUR MONTHLY TAKE-HOME INCOME	MINUS	TOTAL MONTHLY EXPENSES	EQUALS	TOTAL:
$		$		$

This is the amount you have available to save. Does it equal 10% or more? If not, that's OK. Go through your monthly expenses again. Are there places where you can cut down? Would you consider living in a city where housing or transportation costs less? Would you consider biking to work instead of driving? This is where you start juggling things to see which ones are most important. Even if it feels like you can't quite get to 10% for your savings, no matter how much belt-tightening you do, remember that every little bit counts—saving any amount is better than saving nothing at all. As you move on in your career and make more money, reaching that 10% should get easier and easier.

journal

For some people, the idea of creating a budget is worse than getting a root canal. But think of it this way: Creating a balanced budget gives you financial freedom. It's an essential tool to power up your life plan and support your lifestyle. It puts you in control. Use this page to write out your feelings about what that means to you. How does the idea of keeping a budget make you feel?

chapter 5

N ow that you've figured out how to put a little bit of money away, what are you going to do with it? You've got lots of options, but some are smarter than others. Meet Carolina and Ariana.

the SAVING SisTers

Once upon a time, indentical twin sisters Carolina and Ariana decided to save $1,000. Carolina tucked her $1,000 safely away in her underwear drawer. Ariana, on the other hand, put her $1,000 in an interest—bearing savings account. This is the tale of what became of their cash.

{ ONE year later }

How much money do you have saved?

$1,030

A thousand* ... you?

You got $30 just by putting your money in a BANK?

*When you factor in **inflation**, Carolina actually lost money. The $1,000 she saved last year won't buy as much this year.

LOAN APPLICATION
name
address

new CAT

ariana ty

less $

"Actually, I opened a savings account with a credit union through work, and I've earned 3% interest on my $1,000 deposit."

{ Two years later }

Do you *still* have that $1,000 safe in your dresser drawer?

No, now I have $1,158

Yes I do. Do you still have $1,030?

How did you do that?

"Well, I put that $1,030 in a **certificate of deposit**, CD for short. I had to leave it there for two whole years, but I earned 6% interest—twice what it was making in my savings account."

"I started adding $50 to my savings every month, so I saved $600 a year. And I decided to invest. I put half my savings into **bonds** and earned 7% interest. Then I got a **stockbroker** to help me invest the other half in the **stock market**. I put some money into companies I researched and some into **mutual funds**. I earned about 12% on all the **stocks**. I know stocks can be risky, but the stock market pays off over time. You just have to be patient."

Watching Your Money Grow

You saw how Ariana made different kinds of investments over 10 years and how her money grew. Now check out this chart to see how your $1,000 can grow in 20 years.

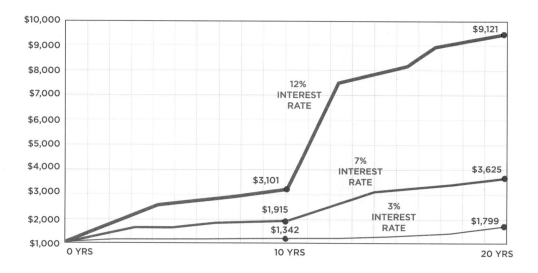

See how the piggy bank and savings account are places where your money makes less than 4% interest? If you save that way, once you factor in inflation, you're actually losing money!

If you started with that $1,000 and saved an additional $50 a month (or $600 a year) as Ariana did, here's how your money could grow over 20 years:

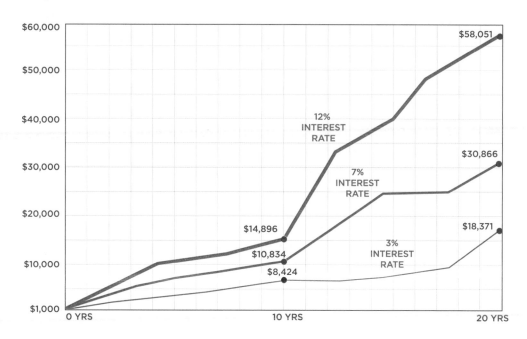

As you can see, if you invested in stocks, you'd have $58,051.

In reality, the growth for stocks and bonds is not smooth. Just like Ariana said, they can lose money over the short term. But after ten or more years, stocks are almost always the best investment.

Even if you don't have a lot of money to invest, you can still make your money grow, thanks to **compounded interest**, which is essentially interest on interest. Suppose you invest $100 in stocks that will earn 10% interest over one year. That $100 is the **principal**, and at the end of one year, it will grow to $110. If you keep your money in those stocks, for the next year you'll earn 10% on $110, so at the end of that year you'll have $121. Get it? In five years you'll have $155. 85; after ten years, you'll have $255.83.

Now imagine how much more your money would grow if you added a little bit each month. If at age 25 you start investing $60 a month in stocks that grow 12% a year, and don't touch that money for 40 years, by the time you're 65, with compounded interest, you'll have one million dollars! (See Chapter 6 for more information about how the stock market works.)

One of the best ways to figure out what to do with your money is to set goals. You can create savings plans with two types of goals:

SHORT-TERM GOALS
for things you want in the near future,
like a computer or a vacation.

LONG-TERM GOALS
for things you want many years from now,
like a new car or a house.

Even though you might not quite be at a point where you're truly ready to start thinking about rent and car loans, it's never too early to start thinking about financial goals.
To get you started, write a few down:

GOAL	SHORT TERM OR LONG TERM

The key to saving for the short term is to find accounts or investments that will give you access to your money when you need it. Savings accounts give you the easiest access to your money, but their interest rates aren't so great. (However, credit union savings accounts usually offer slightly higher interest rates than banks.) Certificates of deposit offer better interest rates than savings accounts, but you have to keep your money in them for a specific amount of time, usually at least three months. Money markets and bonds are also considered good short-term investments, but they usually require a longer commitment than CDs. The bottom line: Once you determine what your saving goals are, do a little research to figure out what savings options make the most sense for you.

Retirement:
Definitely a Long-Term Savings Goal

It may seem a little nutty to be thinking about saving for retirement before you've even started working, but financially savvy girls know that the earlier you begin to save for your golden years, the better. Fortunately, many employers make it very easy. Most offer 401(k) plans, savings plans set up so that a certain amount of money is automatically taken out of your gross earnings and put into an account from which you are not supposed to withdraw until you are 59-and-a-half years old. The money is taxed when you withdraw it, and if you withdraw early, you will also have to pay a penalty.

Some companies even match the amount you contribute to your 401(k). For example, for every dollar you put in, your employer may contribute 50% of that amount to your plan. It's like earning a higher salary with every paycheck. Can you imagine how that could all add up? Something to take advantage of, for sure!

If your employer doesn't offer a retirement plan there are other options. Among the most popular are individual retirement accounts (IRAs). Like 401(k) accounts, IRAs are made up mostly of stocks, bonds, and other investments, and require you to contribute a certain amount of your income. The two primary types of IRAs are:

INDIVIDUAL RETIREMENT ACCOUNT (IRA)

In 2008, you can contribute up to $5,000 of your pre-tax income to a traditional IRA. With this contribution you could be eligible for a $1,000 reduction in your federal income taxes, which is why many people find traditional IRAs attractive. However, because your money is not taxed going into the account, it is taxed when you make a withdrawal. Additionally, except in very specific cases, if you withdraw any money before you're 59-and-a-half years old, you'll have to pay a penalty. And if you don't make any withdrawals by the time you're 70-and-a-half years old, you'll also be penalized.

ROTH IRA

Many financial professionals prefer Roth IRAs to traditional IRAs for several reasons. For one thing, contributions to a Roth come from after-tax income, so you don't pay taxes on the money you withdraw. Plus, you can withdraw the total amount of your contribution without being penalized. Finally, Roth IRAs aren't subject to the same age restrictions as traditional IRAs. In 2008 you can contribute up to $5,000 of your after-tax income to a Roth IRA, but that amount goes up every year, so do your research!

Understanding THE stock MARkeT

DOW
S & P
NASDAQ

BUSINESS JoUrnal

"No dream comes true until you WAKE UP and go to work."

. anonymous.

Chapter 6

From the outside, buildings that house most stock exchanges give little indication of the mayhem within. The centerpiece of every stock exchange is the trading pit, where, at the strike of a bell, people yell, wave their arms wildly, and flash bits of paper at each other. It might look like a party, but if you look closely at those faces, no one really seems to be having a good time (and no one's properly dressed for a fiesta). These frantic people are traders, and they're buying and selling stocks and bonds. Welcome to the stock market.

To stay in business, some companies need people like you to give them money—in other words, to invest in them. This essentially means that you buy a small piece—or **share**—of that company, and in return you get a share of the company's profits. The key is to buy stock (stocks and shares are the same thing) in a company that will do well, so that when you're ready to sell your shares they're worth more than they were when you bought them. The trick is knowing what stocks to keep for the long haul and when to bail out. That's what stockbrokers are for.

To Market, to Market

A good way to understand how the stock market works is to practice investing. Since we're pretending here, just imagine that you have $100,000 to invest in stocks. Why not?

Before you start investing you'll need to pick companies to invest in, do a little research about them, decide how much money to invest in each, then track the performance of your stocks. Not sure how to pick a company? Take a look at your Chapter 1 journal entry. The companies you listed there are companies you know. Since you like their products, why not consider investing in them? For now, pick your favorite five.

STEP 1: BECOMING A SUPER SLEUTH

Before you hand your money over, you definitely want to do some research about the companies you're about to invest in. First, gather some basic information:

- What does the company do?

- Does the company have a product or service that is marketable—in other words, does the company sell something a lot of customers would want to buy?

- Does the company have a commitment to quality?

To dig a little deeper, go to each company's Web site and click on their Investor Relations section. Look at each company's **annual report**. There, you'll find financial statements that can help you answer these questions:

- What is the company's **net income**?

- How does its income this year compare with previous years?

- What are the company's **assets** and **liabilities**?

- How have they changed in recent years?

Look for a Letter to Shareholders to answer these questions:

- What are the company's plans for the future?

- Will it be expanding or restructuring its business?

- Does the company have a successful history?

You can also search the Internet to find out:

- How successful is the company compared to similar companies?

- Has the company recently been in the news?

- What is the company's **market share** in its industry?

STEP 2: TICK, TICK, TICK . . .

Each **publicly owned company** that's traded on the stock market has a **ticker symbol**, which is a three- or four-letter abbreviation that's used to list the company in stock tables. You'll need to know this symbol so you can check the stock tables to see how your company is performing. Here's how to find a company's ticker symbol:

1. Go to the New York Stock Exchange Web site at nyse.com.

2. Click on Symbol Lookup.

3. Type in the name of the company.

Make a list of the companies you're thinking of investing in and their ticker symbols.

COMPANY NAME	TICKER SYMBOL

Ever looked at the business section of a newspaper? Those columns of tiny numbers and abbreviations are a chart that summarizes how much money a company is earning, the current price of its stock, and how that price has changed over a year. Reading stock tables can help you make decisions about investing in a company.

Here's a sample of a stock table listing from the *Wall Street Journal* for the Coca-Cola Company. It shows what went on with Coca-Cola's stock on the previous day.

52-WEEK HIGH AND LOW

HIGH	LOW	STOCK	DIV	YLDPERCENT	P/E	VOL 100S	CLOSE	NET CHG
45.40	39.36	Coca-Cola	$1.24	2.8	20	55211	44.05	- 0.07

THE THREE BIG STOCK EXCHANGES IN THE UNITED STATES ARE

NEW YORK STOCK EXCHANGE (NYSE)

The NYSE is the world's largest stock exchange. (The second largest is Japan's Tokyo Stock Exchange.) It lists about 2,800 companies and 5,000 securities, from large, established businesses to young, high-growth enterprises. It operates from a building on Wall Street using floor traders—that is, actual people. It is also known as the Big Board.

AMERICAN STOCK EXCHANGE (AMEX)

The second largest stock exchange in the United States. It also uses floor traders, but it has less rigid listing requirements than the NYSE, so it attracts smaller companies. It merged with NASDAQ in 1999 but still maintains its name, identity, and separate listings for its stocks.

NATIONAL ASSOCIATION OF SECURITIES DEALERS AUTOMATED QUOTATION SYSTEM (NASDAQ)

The world's fourth largest stock exchange. It lists about 5,000 companies and makes its trades electronically, through computers.

Here's the translation:

52-WEEK HIGH AND LOW: the highest and lowest prices (in dollars) paid for the stock during the past year.

STOCK: the name of the stock, which is sometimes listed in stock tables with its ticker symbol. (Coca-Cola would be KO.)

DIV: the abbreviation for *dividend*. A dividend is the annual dollar amount a shareholder receives from the company's profit for each share owned.

YLDPERCENT: the abbreviation for *yield percentage*. This number is the percentage of the share price the dividend amount represents. In other words, Coca-Cola's $1.24 dividend is 2.8% of the $44.05 share price.

P/E: price/earnings ratio—the price per share of stock is divided by the company's earnings per share for the last year. Some analysts use this number to determine if the share price is too high or too low. Many experts believe that looking at the company's earnings is a better way to see how well it is doing.

VOL 100S: the estimated total number of shares traded on the previous day, with two zeros omitted. In this example 5,521,100 shares were traded.

CLOSE: the final price (or closing price) paid for the stock on the previous day.

NET CHG: the difference between the closing price of the stock and the price of the stock on the day before that. In this example, Coca-Cola shares went down seven cents a share.

Check out the stock tables for each of the companies you're considering investing in. How do your companies' current prices (the close amounts) compare with the 52-week high and low prices listed in the stock tables?

Take a few weeks to read stock tables for your companies before you make your investment choices. You can also check Web sites to see how the companies' stocks have been performing in recent months. That will give you a sense of how much their prices fluctuate.

Keep a record of your research. The information you gather from the annual report, from reading the stock tables, from various other resources, including your own feelings about the companies, will help you determine what companies you really want to invest in. For example, here's what your research report on Apple, Inc. might look like:

APPLE, INC.
TICKER SYMBOL: AAPL

WHAT I KNOW

- Makes computers, software, iPods, and iPhones.
- In business for many years and has lots of loyal customers.
- The Mac I use at school is of real high quality. And I love my iPod!
- New innovations like the iPhone keep Apple on the cutting edge.

WHAT I LEARNED FROM THE ANNUAL REPORT (NUMBERS IN MILLIONS):

YEAR	NET INCOME	ASSETS	LIABILITIES
2003	$69	$6,815	$2,592
2004	$276	$8,050	$2,974
2005	$1,335	$11,551	$4,085
2006	$1,993	$17,244	$6,456

Other Things from the Annual Report:

· U.S. sales increased 64% in 2006 compared to 2004.

· They expect fluctuation in their future earnings. One reason their earnings may be negatively affected is their plan to change to Intel-based technology.

· They are committed to research and development, especially because they know competitors will be coming out with products to compete with the iPod.

What I Learned from News Reports and Internet Searches:

· Most recent 4th quarter profit report announced a net profit of $546 million compared to $430 million in the 4th quarter of 2005. CNN Money reports iPod sales are up 35% from the previous year.

· Apple recently announced they were going to refresh their line of iPod MP3 players.

· Los Angeles Times article says that Sony and Microsoft both plan to compete with the iPod.

· Apple's market share in the personal computer industry is between 2 and 4.7%.

- Hewlett Packard is the #1 U.S. company for PC sales—it recently took first place over Dell.

- HP and Dell have had steady growth in sales in recent years, though their stocks have been volatile. Right now Dell's stock prices are falling, and HP's are rising.

From AAPL Stock Tables:

- 52-week high/low: $86.40/$50.16

- Most recent close (Oct 20, 2006): $79.95

- Two weeks ago: $74.42

- High of $86.40 was last January—ten months ago

- Low of $50.16 was last July—three months ago

STEP 4: CREATING YOUR STOCK PORTFOLIO

Now that you've researched your companies, choose five you'd most like to invest in and list them in the chart on page 75. These stocks make up your portfolio. Don't be concerned if you're not absolutely sure which stocks will make you money. Doing your research will help, but even experienced investors will tell you that there are no 100% guarantees when it comes to the stock market. To cover yourself, it's always a good idea to invest in a variety of stocks. In other words, you might want to invest in established companies that have solid money-making records and take a chance on newer companies that make products you really like. Mixing it up like this is known as diversifying your portfolio.

Now for the fun part! If you were buying stocks for real, you'd be working with a stockbroker, but for now, you'll make your own investments. How should you spend your money? It's up to you. Think about your goals. Are they long-term or short-term? Do you want to see your money grow over time, or do you want to make as much money as you can as quickly as possible? Your research will tell you which stocks are riskier than others, which are steady climbers, and which are projected to quickly increase in value. There's no wrong answer here, and since we're just pretending, why not try a few things just to see what you learn?

To help you decide where to put your money, you might want to figure out how far it will go. To calculate how many shares of a company your money will buy, use this equation:

$$\frac{Total\ amount\ of\ money\ invested}{Share\ price} = Total\ number\ of\ shares\ you've\ purchased.$$

Congratulations! You hold stock in five companies!

Since the stock market is highly volatile (stock prices can go up and down depending on a lot of factors), the best strategy is to keep money in your stocks for several years.

MY STOCK PORTFOLIO   DATE:

COMPANY NAME	TICKER SYMBOL	SHARE PRICE	MY INVESTMENT	NUMBER OF SHARES I OWN

MY TOTAL INVESTMENT $100,000

What does it mean when you hear "The stock market went up" or "The stock market went down"?

These are reports about what's going on with the **Dow Jones Industrial Average**. The Dow is a stock **index**. It measures the average activities of 30 of the largest companies that trade in the stock market. Many financial experts say that the Dow doesn't really give a true picture of what's going on, because it deals with so few companies. Another popular index is called **Standard & Poor's 500**. This index measures 500 companies. Because it deals with more companies, financial experts see it as a more accurate report on stock market activity.

STEP 5: WATCHING YOUR COMPANIES PERFORM

Now all you have to do is sit back and watch the market, either online or in the newspaper. For the next six months, track the progress of your stocks. Are they losing money, gaining, or staying the same?

At the end of six months, record the current share price of the stock and write it down in the chart below. Then write the current value of your investment in each stock in the My Investment column. Add up your My Investment column to get your total investment amount.

MY STOCK PORTFOLIO
SIX MONTHS LATER

DATE:

COMPANY NAME	TICKER SYMBOL	SHARE PRICE	MY INVESTMENT	NUMBER OF SHARES I OWN
MY TOTAL INVESTMENT			$	

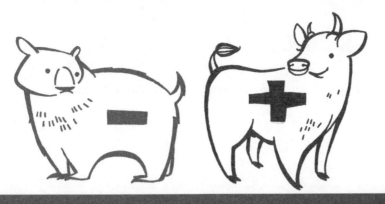

Taking Stock

Now that you've taken a tour of the stock market, it's time to evaluate. What happened to your total investment? Is your current total more than $100,000? Less? Which companies made money? Which companies lost money? Have any stayed pretty much the same? Do the results surprise you? Did your research and notes help you to discover the reasons why your stocks gained or lost money? Were there events in the news that caused your stock prices to rise or fall? Answering these questions will help you figure out how to make future investments. There's a lot more to learn about the ins and outs of the stock market so when you're ready to really invest, check out the resources at the end of this book for more information.

Bravo! You've taken a walk down Wall Street and taken the first steps toward becoming market savvy.

journal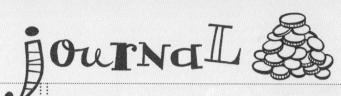

What did you learn from investing in the stock market?

How did it feel when your stocks lost money?

Are you comfortable with the thought of losing money, even if you know you're likely to make that money back in the long run?

When you're ready to invest for real, understanding how losing money in the market makes you feel will help you determine how comfortable you are making risky investments.

CHapter 7

R emember Maria and her dog walking business? It's 12 years later and Maria's pooch patrol days are long gone. But she's still as ambitious as ever. Take a look:

"*The important thing is not being afraid to take a chance.*
Remember, the greatest failure is to not try.
Once you find something you love to do, be the best at doing it."

—DEBBI FIELDS, FOUNDER OF MRS. FIELDS,
A COMPANY SHE CREATED IN 1977 WHEN SHE WAS 20 YEARS OLD

later

A few days later Maria takes a batch of maple bars to Regina's Café, where Regina herself samples them.

ONE year later

Six stores in Maria's neighborhood are selling her maple bars! She'd like to expand her business, but she can't afford to do it on her own.

Two years later

FouR years later

Maria is so nationally successful she plans to build more stores.

{TEN years later}

Maria has started a new line of
low-calorie maple bars.

"What's really great is that now my mom only
works part time and Grandma is finally retiring.
And I've started a mentoring program
to teach teen girls about how to start their
own businesses."

IPO or No?

If getting to Wall Street is as easy as Maria and Rosa make it seem, why isn't every sidewalk lemonade stand being traded on the New York Stock Exchange? First of all, going public can be expensive, so little Lucy Lemonade would have to squeeze an awful lot of lemons to become Lucy, Inc. (By the way, "inc." at the end of a business name means the business is a legally recognized group that includes shareholders.)

Secondly, once your company makes that **initial public offering** (also known as an IPO), it's not just you calling the shots anymore. Every stockholder owns a little bit of your business, and sometimes that means they have a say in how your company is run. Plus, having shareholders means you have to share your company's profits with them. And all of the financial reporting your company will have to do might tip off the competition to your fantastic new ideas. Some companies (and entrepreneurs) just aren't into being so . . . public.

On the other hand, there are many benefits to going public. The most obvious one is that it feels pretty good to know that your company is successful enough for people to want to invest in. Those investments will generate capital that will keep your company up and running. Your employees can also benefit when you go public. Lots of companies offer **stock options** in additional to salaries. This means that at an agreed-upon time in the future—say, after two years of employment—an employee can buy shares of your company for a set price. If, when the time comes for the employee to buy, the value of the shares has increased beyond the set price (which, of course, is the hope), the employee makes a nice little profit.

advisors

How to Get to Wall Street

By the time you're ready to go public, you'll probably have a whole team of advisors to tell you what you need to do when, so we won't go into great detail here. But the very first step is usually to register your company with the Securities and Exchange Commission (SEC). The SEC is a government group that oversees the buying and selling of stocks and bonds (together known as securities) and protects investors from any wrongdoing. When you register, you'll have to describe your company, provide financial documents, and explain who your competitors are, among other things. Once this process is underway, you're on your way to Wall Street!

JOuRNaL

If you started your own business would you want to take it public? Why or why not?

"I have found that among its other benefits, giving liberates the SOUL of the giver."
·Maya Angelou·
poet

giving BACK

chapter 8

One of the best things about making good choices when it comes to earning, managing, and investing your money is this: You'll be living a life where you can choose to give something back to the world to make it a better place. You'll have the power to use some of your time, talents, and money to help change things you believe need changing for the better. When you do this, you are a **philanthropist**.

> **PHILANTHROPIST:**
> *someone who works to increase the well-being of humankind through charitable actions or donations.*

Effortless Giving

Many businesses use a portion of their profits to create foundations that help others in their local area and in the global community. In fact, many companies have recently given lots of money to assist the victims of the Southeast Asian tsunami and Hurricane Katrina, so buying things from these corporations is an easy way to give back. Here's a partial list of which companies are doing what. (Do a little digging to find out what other companies are giving back.)

The Gap helps underprivileged children all over the world by donating money to provide them with food, health care, and after-school programs.

Levi Strauss & Co. funds the Asia Foundation project, which helps migrant women workers in China improve their workplace rights, financial literacy, and health care.

Microsoft donates products and pays for educational programs around the globe so people can improve their lives through technology.

Macy's has created a Vendor Development Program that helps businesses that are owned by women and minorities.

The Limited established The Giving Tree, which helps needy families all over the nation and provides books for children to improve literacy.

Nonprofit organizations are created for specific causes, such as fighting poverty, finding cures for diseases, or bringing art to communities. They receive donations from businesses, other foundations, government institutions, and individuals who believe in supporting their causes. Nonprofit organizations often give **grants** to groups or individuals to further the work they are doing. Charities and religious organizations—along with some government groups, hospitals, schools, and art and research institutions—are supported by nonprofit organizations. Each nonprofit has a specific mission, and the great thing about most of them is that you can make a donation or volunteer to help with their causes:

Meals on Wheels works to deliver food to people who are homebound.

The Metropolitan Museum of Art was established to encourage and develop the study and appreciation of fine art.

Women's Foundation of California supports the equity for and the advancement of women and girls in California by improving their economic security, health, and opportunities for leadership development.

In fact, this book, *It's a Money Thing!*, is just one of the many projects of the Women's Foundation of California. It was created to help girls like you learn financial literacy skills so that you can lead lives in which your money is working for you.

> For more information about the
> Women's Foundation of California, check out
> **WWW.WOMENSFOUNDCA.ORG.**

How can I make the world a better place — right now?

Volunteering

Sometimes it's not your money that's needed but your time. Volunteering is a great way to give back, especially if you feel that you really can't afford to donate money. Plus, you can learn a lot from your experiences as a volunteer. For example, if you're interested in a career in medicine, you can volunteer at a hospital and find out what it would be like to spend your days doing what health-care workers do. Or you might help out at a local theater and see if the world of entertainment excites you. You could even work to help get someone elected into public office and learn all kinds of things about the government. Once you start looking around, you're sure to discover that volunteering is a two-way street—as you help others, the experience will enrich your life, too.

> **GRANT:**
> *an award of money given to an organization or individual for a specific purpose.*

Nonprofit organizations are exempt from income taxes (meaning they don't pay them), since all of the money donated is used in support of their cause and for their operating expenses, and none is kept for profit. When you give money to a nonprofit organization you become a part of the tax-exempt struc-ture. That means you can report how much you donated on your income tax form as a tax-deductible donation.

No matter how you choose to share your time, talent, and money with the world around you, every action you take to make the world a better place will help you grow into a happier, stronger, better person, too!

Here are some Web sites you can check out to learn about other volunteer opportunities:

dosomething.org
volunteermatch.org
joinhandsday.org
ysa.org

journal

Imagine yourself ten years from now. How will you be using your time, talents, and money as a philanthropist?

Feels good to be financially savvy, doesn't? Now you can talk bears, bulls, and certificates of deposit with the best of 'em. But much, much better than that, you're on your way to becoming a woman who knows how to manage her money.

Of course, there's a lot more to learn than we could possibly hold in the pages of this book. Below are a few resources that will point you in the right direction. Best of luck!

WEB SITES

escapefromknab.com
A game where financial decision-making skills are used to earn a spaceship ticket that will take players home from the planet Knab.

fantasystockmarket.com
An interactive way to learn about investing and the stock market.

finance.yahoo.com
Provides current stock quotes and articles about the stock market, personal finance, and the economy.

independentmeans.com
The leading provider of financial educational products and programs in the United States.

ja.org
Site for the Junior Achievement organization, providing information about their 150 programs in the United States that teach high school students about business and economics.

moneycentral.msn.com
Provides current stock quotes and articles about the stock market, personal finance, and the economy.

nyse.com
The official site of the New York Stock Exchange.

taapslink.gov/sav/savkids.htm
Provides information about savings bonds.

smgww.org
An interactive stock market game that requires registration and a fee to play.

strongkids.com
Provides resources and information on investing and making money.

younginvestor.com
Includes sections for teens, kids, parents, and teachers with easy-to-understand financial information and games.

youngmoney.com
A business and lifestyle magazine for young adults that focuses on money management, careers, investing, technology, travel, entertainment, and automotive topics.

The Complete Idiot's Guide to Personal Finance in Your 20s & 30s, by Sarah Young Fisher and Susan Shelly; Penguin Group (2005)

Empowered Girls: A Girl's Guide to Positive Activism, Volunteering, and Philanthropy, by Frances A. Karnes and Kristen R. Stephens; Prufrock Press Inc. (2004)

The Martha Rules, by Martha Stewart; Martha Stewart Living Omnimedia, Inc. (2005)

The Money Book for the Young, Fabulous & Broke, by Suze Orman; Riverhead Hardcover (2005)

Money Makeovers: How Women Can Control Their Financial Destiny, by Christopher L. Hayes and Kate Kelly; Main Street Books (1999)

No More Frogs to Kiss: 99 Ways to Give Economic Power to Girls, by Joline Godfrey; Harper Collins (1995)

Our Wildest Dreams: Women Entrepreneurs Making Money, Having Fun, Doing Good, by Joline Godfrey; Harper Business (1992)

Prince Charming Isn't Coming: How Women Get Smart About Money, by Barbara Stanny; Penguin Books (1999)

Rich Dad Poor Dad for Teens: The Secrets About Money—That You Don't Learn in School, by Robert T. Kiyosaki and Sharon L. Lechter; Little Brown Young Readers (2004)

Smart Women Finish Rich: 9 Steps to Achieving Financial Security and Funding Your Dreams, by Richard Bach; Broadway (2002)

The Teenage Investor, by Timothy Olsen; McGraw Hill (2003)

Testing the Waters: A Teen's Guide to Career Exploration, by Alice N. Culbreath and Saundra K. Neal; Jrc Consulting (1999)

Twenty Secrets to Money and Independence: The Dollar Diva's Guide to Life, by Joline Godfrey; St. Martin's Griffin (2000)

What Color Is Your Parachute for Teens: Discovering Yourself, Defining Your Future, by Richard Nelson Bolles, Carol Christen, Jean M. Blomquist; Ten Speed Press (2006)

glossary

ANNUAL REPORT: a document that contains financial as well as other information about how a company is doing and what it plans to do in the future.

ANNUAL PERCENTAGE RATE: a yearly percentage of a loan, used to calculate interest.

ASSET: any possession that has value in an exchange. For example, financial assets could include stocks and bonds, and physical assets could include a car or a house.

BALANCE: an amount in excess, especially on the credit side of a financial account. For example, if you pay off only a portion of your credit card, the balance is the amount left to be paid.

BEAR MARKET: a period of time when stock prices are falling.

BOND: a certificate that represents a long-term debt of a government or corporation. When you buy a bond you loan an institution money to pay part of their debt and they agree to pay you back with interest at a specified time.

BUDGET: a financial plan that summarizes income, expenses, and savings over a period of time. A budget is balanced when your income equals the amount you spend (including 10% of your income for savings).

BULL MARKET: a period of time when stock prices are rising.

CAPITAL: money and supplies that help a business grow.

CASH RESERVE: money that a business sets aside to cover future expenses or possible losses.

CERTIFICATE OF DEPOSIT (CD): a certificate that can be purchased from a bank or savings institution. CDs require that a set amount of money be kept in the CD for a specified period of time (usually a minimum of six months). The money is guaranteed to be repaid at a fixed rate of interest.

COMPOUNDED INTEREST: interest on the initial investment amount and on the interest that initial amount earns.

CREDIT: a loan of money. Also the ability to borrow money to purchase things in exchange for a promise to pay later.

CREDIT CARD: a card given to you by a business or a bank so that you can borrow money from them. In exchange for the loan, you agree to pay them back and pay them a fee for loaning you the money.

CREDIT UNION: a financial group whose members share either the same place of employment or the same labor union. Like a bank, a credit union offers its members loans as well as savings plans with interest.

DEBIT CARD: a card that looks like a credit card but which is used to take money out of your savings or checking account right at the moment the card is used.

DEBT: the amount of money you owe.

DIVIDENDS: the part of a company's earnings that is distributed to shareholders. Also called a "payout."

DOW JONES INDUSTRIAL AVERAGE (THE DOW): a stock index that measures the average activities of 30 of the largest companies that trade in the stock market. Many financial experts say that the Dow doesn't really give a true picture of what's going on, because it deals with so few companies.

ENTREPRENEUR: a person who takes a risk to create a new product or service, or to develop a better way to do something.

GRANT: an award of money given to an organization or individual for a specific purpose.

GROSS INCOME: money earned before tax deductions are calculated.

INCOME TAX: a tax (or sum of money, calculated as a percentage) on the total earnings of an individual or company.

INDEX: a statistical measure of change in the stock market or economy.

INFLATION: the rate at which prices rise and the purchasing power of the dollar falls. For example, with a 2% inflation rate, a candy bar that costs $1 this year will cost $1.02 next year.

INITIAL PUBLIC OFFERING (IPO): a company's first offer to sell stock to the public.

INTEREST: a fee for the privilege of borrowing money, most often calculated as a percentage, which is called an interest rate. For example, a credit card company could charge you an 18% interest rate on your purchases. Or a bank could pay you 3% interest on your savings.

LIABILITY: the amount of money an individual or a company owes.

MARKET RESEARCH: the collection and analysis of information about consumers and market niches, and the effectiveness of advertising strategies.

MARKET SHARE: a brand's share of the total sales of all products within the product category in which the brand competes. For example, Coca-Cola has a large market share in the soft-drink industry.

MISSION STATEMENT: a written description of a company that clearly outlines its purpose, and sometimes its goals.

MUTUAL FUND: an investment fund that contains a collection of different stocks or bonds. Because each part of the collection can gain and lose money at different times, a mutual fund aims to be a balanced investment and is not as risky as investing in individual stocks.

NET INCOME: in business, the dollar amount that is left after expenses are subtracted from income, also called net profits. In personal finance, gross income minus tax deductions.

NET PROFITS: the dollar amount that is left after a business subtracts its expenses from its income.

NET WORTH: the amount of money calculated by subtracting what you owe (your liabilities) from what you have (your assets).

PHILANTHROPIST: someone who works to increase the well-being of humankind through charitable actions or donations.

PRINCIPAL: the original investment amount or the amount of a loan that equals the amount that was borrowed, without interest.

PRIVATE COMPANY: a company that is usually owned by its founders or a small group of investors. Its financial budgets are not approved by the Securities and Exchange Commission (SEC), so shares of the company cannot be offered to the general public.

PUBLICLY OWNED COMPANY: a company that has been approved by the Securities and Exchange Commission (SEC) to sell shares (also called stock) of itself to the general public.

SHARE: a unit of partial ownership in a corporation, or stock.

SHAREHOLDER: a person who owns shares (also called stock) in a corporation.

STANDARD & POOR'S 500 (S&P 500): a stock index that measures 500 companies. Financial experts see it as a more accurate report on stock market activity than the Dow.

STOCK: a share of ownership in a company. If a company is successful, its stock can be worth a lot of money.

STOCKBROKER: a person who buys and sells stocks for others and earns a commission or fee for this service.

STOCK MARKET: the organized market for trading stocks. Also called the equity market.

STOCK OPTIONS: the right to purchase shares in a company for an agreed-upon price.

TAKE-HOME PAY: the money your employer pays you after income taxes and various other expenses are taken out.

VENTURE CAPITALIST: someone who lends money to help a business that is just starting up or expanding.

WALL STREET: the street on which the New York Stock Exchange, considered the center of American finance, is located.

iNDeX

Book design by Allison Henry.
The illustrations in this book were rendered digitally and by hand.
Production assistance by Adam Osgood.
Manufactured in China.

Library of Congress Cataloging-in-Publication Data
It's a money thing! : a girl's guide to managing money / by The Women's
Foundation of California ; illustrated by Susan Estelle Kwas.
p. cm.
Previously published: It's a money thing : a money planner for teenage girls /
by The Los Angeles Women's Foundation. c2005. With revisions and new illustrations.
Includes bibliographical references.
ISBN 978-0-8118-4427-7
1. Girls—Finance, Personal—Juvenile literature. 2. Teenage girls—Finance,
Personal—Juvenile literature. 3. Investments—Juvenile literature. I. Kwas, Susan
Estelle.
II. Women's Foundation of California. III. Title: Girl's guide to managing money.
HG179.I876 2008
332.02400835'2—dc22
2007013134

10 9 8 7 6 5 4 3 2 1

Chronicle Books LLC
680 Second Street, San Francisco, California 94107

www.chroniclekids.com